MOGUE
The Prehistoric Genius

NATE WREY

Illustrated by
Helen Cochrane

Published in 2022 by Waterman Books

Copyright © Nate Wrey 2022

Nate Wrey has asserted his right to be identified as the author of this Work in accordance with the Copyright, Designs and Patents Act 1988

ISBN Paperback: 978-1-9163705-4-8
Ebook: 978-1-9163705-5-5

All rights reserved. No part of this publication may be reproduced, stored in a retrieval system, or transmitted in any form or by any means, electronic, mechanical, photocopying, recording or otherwise, without the prior permission of the copyright owner.

All characters and events in this publication, other than those clearly in the public domain, are fictitious and any resemblance to real persons, living or dead,
is purely coincidental.

A CIP catalogue copy of this book can be found
in the British Library.

Published with the help of Indie Authors World
www.indieauthorsworld.com

To those that once read to me and for Joseph

Acknowledgments

With thanks to my family, David Ashley, Mary Whinder, Jane Manning, Zoe and Charlotte Ward, Jessica Ashley, the children from Mayflower Primary School, Harwich, Sprites Primary Academy, Ipswich, Miles Hawksley from Daniel Goldsmith Associates, Kim Macleod and all from Indie Authors World and, of course, Helen Cochrane

Contents

Introduction	9
Nothing	12
Tools	17
Fire	22
Clothes	27
Art	32
Animals	36
The Wheel	41
The Boat	47
Ceramics	51
Pickling and Preserving	56
Bread	62
Farming	66
Writing	71
Timeline and Facts	77
About the Author	81

Introduction

How clever we are to fly in the sky,

To build grand buildings that reach so high.

For these and all the things in our time,

We thank those smarty-pants who shine,

Through invention, discovery, heart and courage;

All those ideas that build our knowledge.

Now go back in time, to days of old,

When others lived whose brains, I'm told,

Unlocked secrets while risking it all.

Helping humans to stand so tall.

And back and back and back we go,

When mammoths roamed through lots of snow.

Where in a cave, or so it's said,

Lived the genius Mooge, long now dead.

The first to discover, the first to invent.

He started it all: the human ascent.

Mooge's not famous, as you probably know,

For he lived such a long time ago:

Not one century back, not even two,

But centuries of centuries. Honest! It's true!

Please don't yet clap or sing his praise.

I've tales to tell which may well raise

An eyebrow or two, or hearty laugh.

Prepare yourself for something daft!

For with all the improvements humans have made,

A mistake or luck has come to our aid.

So, read on to see in every rhyme,

That old Mooge was the luckiest of all time.

Nothing

Or

Nothing x Nothing = Nothing

A long, long, VERY long time ago
It was rather cold with lots of snow.
Upon the land roamed beasts with hair,
Some quite big and designed to scare.

With claws so sharp and snarling nose,
And fangs and teeth to chew on those
Who wandered out without a jot,
As humans did not possess a lot.

They had no phones, bikes, or steel.

Clothes, tools or fire, not even the wheel!

All did struggle in this age of ice,

Where staying warm was rare but nice.

And finding food was the hardest thing,

You never knew what tomorrow would bring.

Now, Mooge lived at this horrid time:

A man quite small, though big on grime.

He wandered afar in search of food,

With family in tow, all completely nude.

"I'm hungry!" he moaned, as was his way,

As they trudged along through sticky clay.

When up before them a piglet stopped,

Missing one leg, most definitely crocked.

"Food!" gasped Mooge, his eyes aglow,

As he looked around for a thing to throw.

With nothing there but mud and ice,

He turned around to seek advice.

So, now's the time to welcome Flair,

The wife of Mooge, with jet black hair.

She urged him on with a prod and wave

"Leap on it, Mooge! Be big and brave."

Mooge licked his lips and tried to budge,

But with feet stuck firm he fell in the sludge.

The piglet oinked and limped away:

Gone was their food for another day.

Mooge sat up straight with a soggy squelch,

Letting out a hungry belch.

"This can't go on!" Flair sobbed with a curse,

When a lion approached to make things worse.

"Run!" screamed Flair, as all turned tail,

Except our Mooge, who just went pale.

The big beast paused to give some thought

To the skinny man it had caught.

But with a snooty look, walked on through:

This man with no meat wouldn't do!

So, Mooge was saved but not best pleased,

As he shivered with fear and then sneezed.

He located Flair hiding up a tree:
The safest place for humans to be.
"This can't go on!" Flair cried once more.
"We can't even catch a three-legged boar.
We'll die without a better way
To live our lives day by day.
We shiver with cold and shake with fright.
When danger comes, we just take flight."
Mooge nodded his head, as he did with Flair.
He never argued: he didn't dare.
"I'll work it out. Just give me time,"
Promised Flair as she began to climb
Down from the tree, on to the snow,
where an idea formed and started to grow.
"Do you see those holes in the cliff,
Beyond the swamp?" she said with a sniff.
"They're out of the wind and free of ice.
Good for protection. They look quite nice.
Let's stay there whenever we can:
A place of safety where we can plan!"

With all agreed, they set off at a jog,

Being careful to avoid the bog.

Except our Mooge, who couldn't wait,

Dashing ahead. Splash! Too late!

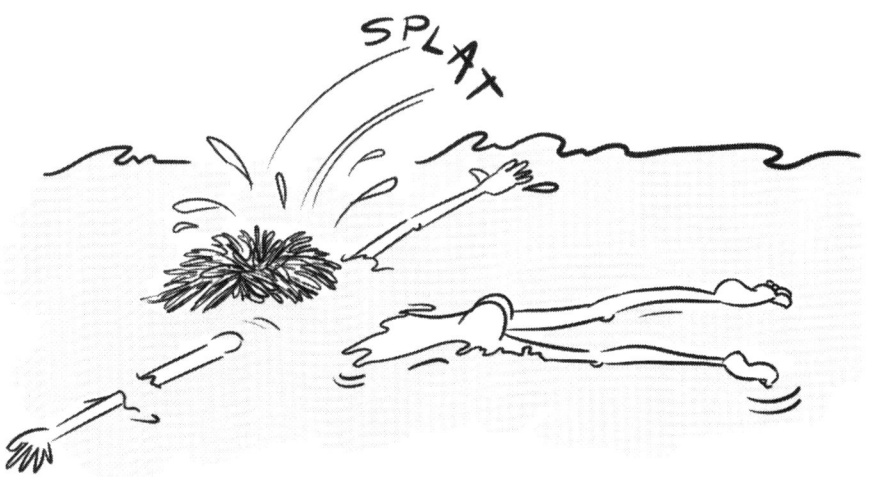

They weren't much, these humble caves,

For humans with nothing, and yet it paves

The way towards our next daft rhyme,

By showing the challenges of this time.

Will poor humanity rise or fall?

Read on, dear reader, to discover all.

Tools

or

How Mooge Used His Head to Make Tools

"There isn't much to do," thought Mooge,
"Just not get eaten or look for food."
So, he sat within his cold, dark cave,
Fingers twiddling, his beard unshaved.

But then an idea arose within,
To save on time and provide a trim.
A 'thing' was needed to do his work,
To ease his load and let him shirk.
Mooge eyed a stone upon the floor,
Round and plain, once thrown at boar,
But not much help to snip or clip.
He picked it up and moaned, "Oh, flip!"
Then threw it with a careless neglect,
Skimming the ceiling, to then deflect

Down to the floor, then up in the air,
Hitting his wife, you remember, Flair.

She cursed a word or two in pain,
And lobbed it back at Mooge again.
Glancing off his heavy brow,
It hit the wall, as he cried "Ow!"

'Crack!' and 'bang!' went the sound,
Of breaking stone upon the ground.
Mooge just shrugged, his mind daydreaming,
While Flair cleaned up, her mind seething.

"Ouch!" She withdrew her hand at speed,
A shard of flint had made her bleed.
Its sharp, black edge had hurt her pinkie.
"What more do you cut, oh stone?" thinks she.
"Could I skin deer, chop down a tree,
Trim Mooge's beard, or make jewellery?"

A big smile formed. She saw it all.
"I'll call this handy thing a 'tool'!"
Her cry stirred Mooge from absent thought.
He scratched his hair and gave a snort,
"I've had an idea to change your life,
Called it the Stone Swish Army Knife.
Pieces of flint stuck in a wood rod,
For stones upon which the deer have trod,
They're crying out for a thing that removes
Those rocks that get stuck in their hooves.

Not a bad idea and most humane,"

Said Mooge, having exhausted his brain.

Flair rolled her eyes, as she readied for bed,

And threw a stone at Mooge's sore head.

If she had to put up with this hairy fool,

Then at least he could help make another tool.

And over time, after long hours spent

On new materials and experiment,

They had lots of tools to help them out,

Like flint stone axes and a flibbleout.

You don't know what a flibbleout does?

Why, it's to swat those things that annoy and buzz.

It didn't last - was gone in a blink -

After Mooge made one but didn't think.

That piece of wood with stone bound-tight

Was good at squashing things that bite.

But when a fly landed on Flair's nose…

Well, you can guess what happened next, I suppose?

Fire

or

How A Bright Spark Learned the Secret of Fire

In Summer's short burst of lovely heat,
With snow thawed and food to eat,
Mooge walked across the sun-drenched land,
A flint-tipped spear held firm in hand.

Upon his back a big boar lay.
They wouldn't starve on this fine day.
By his side strode Uncle Pel,
Old and hairy, with a fruity smell.
Home was just beyond the hill,
Where others waited to have their fill
Of berries, roots, and fresh, raw meat,
Or anything else that they could eat.

But high above came a darkened cloud,
The sun blocked out, the sky cried loud,
As rain plopped down, deliciously cool,
Before it then turned torrential.
Afraid and cold, Mooge found some cover,
While Uncle Pel just didn't bother.
"It's dry under my tree," Mooge joked,
Laughing out loud as Pel got soaked.
Until a clap, a flash and sizzle,
Turned Mooge's hair a crispy frizzle.

Then smoke escaped through mouth and ears.

He screamed aloud and cried some tears.

"Ho! Ho!" Uncle Pel laughed with glee.

"You never hide beneath a tree.

The clouds will get you with their flame,

They spot a fool and then take aim."

A rattled Mooge ignored the quip,

While hissing from a fallen drip.

"Let's get going! Home's not far,"

He growled just like a jaguar.

So, on they went along their path,

The silence broken by old Pel's laugh.

And finally, with home in sight,

Their families waved: their smiles all bright.

"So, my new spear worked a treat?" Flair sung,

Spotting the boar, and where it hung.

"But what is that unusual smell?"

As all eyes turned to Uncle Pel.

"No, not the pong of stinky feet.

It smells delicious enough to eat."

Mooge dropped the boar on to the grass,

His finger scratching upon his sparse,

Frazzled hair atop his nog,

As he looked upon the roasted hog.

"Our meat is ruined. It's not my fault.

I nearly did a somersault.

A flame attacked me from the sky.

I couldn't breathe; I thought I'd die.

My bits are singed; my hair a mess.

The boar has crisped, I must confess."

Now not a girl to let things go,

Flair bent her knees to sniff below.

The rich aroma of sizzled boar

Teased her nose; she wanted more.

She plucked a piece of tender meat,

And popped it in her drooling cheek.

"Mmm" she crooned, the taste entrancing,

A probing tongue, her brown eyes dancing.

"The heat has made this boar a dream.

Mixed with honey it'll taste supreme."

But then she stopped in near defeat.
"Can I recreate this magic heat?"
Mooge, who was no help at all,
Brushed his hair with his new flint tool.
"We'll call it 'fire' and this meat 'fried',
Decided Flair, as she took a stride.
"Now go and eat," she urged with a wink.
"I'll rub two sticks. It helps me think."
And as Flair thought, stick rubbing stick,
Try guessing what then happened. Quick!
That's right. The wood first smoked, then it burned,
And that's how the secret of fire was learned.

Clothes

or

How Mooge No Longer Had to Bare His Soul...or Bottom.

A snowflake landed on Mooge's nose,

As icy wind disturbed his doze.

Rubbing his arms to keep them warm

Was useless in this bitter storm.

At least the fire now gave some heat.

He shifted round to toast his feet.

His naked form, though covered in hair,

Shivered in the freezing air.

So, he rose and stood above the flame:

A risky act with things to maim.

When naughty sparks dared to leap,

Landing where one can never speak.

Mooge screamed and danced around in pain,

His curly hair now one big flame.

But with mind so sharp and nifty feet,
Flair threw some snow to cool the heat.
The burning glow on Mooge's bare tum
Hissed and smoked: his belly numb.
"Phew!" he sighed, with groans and tuts,
Whilst bending down to roast some nuts.
Flair seemed lost in deep reflection.
"What we need is some protection."
She spied some skins beyond the smoke,
Beginning to picture a lovely cloak.
"With one snip here and one cut there,
I could make some frilly underwear.
While fur against my tender skin,
Will stop the cold from getting in."
Then she set to making clothes,
While Mooge just sat and picked his nose.
And once complete, she dressed all out
In skins with which to preen and pout.
Clad in grey old Pel felt nice,
Then learned he shared his fur with mice.

And baby Bur began to purr,

All bundled up in lovely fur.

But what of Mooge who inspired his girl?

Well, he loved his fur and gave a swirl,

Then stood upon some glassy ice.

The faint reflection looked so nice.

But when he moved, it cracked like thunder,

The ice then split, and he fell under.

Once more Flair shouted, 'Oh, you fool!'

And rescued him from the freezing pool.

So back they went to cave and fire,

To thaw Mooge out and get him drier.

Then one step closer, he stood astride,

To feel the fire's warmth inside,

Ignoring his wife, who gasped and spoke,

"Don't...!" Too late! Mooge went up in smoke!

Art
or

How Mooge Brought Up the Idea of Art

With fire and tools at his command,

And dressed in slippers while socks were darned,

Mooge felt the world a better place,

Just see the smile upon his face.

The winters felt a little less cold.

The food now tasted not so old.

His chin was even free of hair,

Though scarred with cuts so not quite bare.

But back to this story, this silly rhyme.

I must now tell you of the time,

When Mooge, with all his usual grace,

Invented art to brighten the place.

Their cave was not a pretty one,

All dark with mould and bugs and dung.

Then one fine day without a name,

Flair cooked a meal to try new game.

Brought back by Mooge from a long, hard hunt,
It was nothing more than a tiny runt.
She had named the beast Rattus Rat,
And dropped it in her large shell vat.

Stewing with some herbs and fruit,
Flair stirred while adding grated root.
Then slopped it in a flint-carved bowl,
And yelled for Mooge to fill his hole.
He took the meal and kicked a bone,
With one hand resting on cold stone.
Suck, slurp, guzzle: he wolfed it all,
Then spewed some out upon the wall.
"Yuck!" he cried. "What's in that stew?
"It looks okay but tastes like..."
He never finished his meaty moan.
Flair cut him short with her steely tone.

"Move your hand!" came the firm, loud call.
"What patterns lie upon the wall?"
Her husband did as he was told,
To find his hand outlined in bold,
Upon the wall, surrounded by stew:
All rather pretty with a peculiar hue.

"Now, imagine what we could do,"
Chirped Flair, "with yellow, red or blue!
How pretty our little cave would be
With hands, and beasts we want for tea."
Mooge burped, then turned a sickly green.
A guggle guggled from a place unseen.
What little he'd swallowed off his plate,
Now came back up to decorate
His dear wife, poor suffering Flair,
Who screamed in fury at her ruined hair.
Then stopped to wonder, examining it,
How some carrot appeared in Mooge's vomit.

From that time on, they covered their wall,
With hands and beasts, big and small.
Using burnt bones and ground up stone,
Applied with sticks or chewed and blown.
And if they hunted deer or duck,
They'd paint one on to give them luck.
Mooge's drawn ducks were really swell,
Which meant he caught a lot as well.
But he never did catch the wild bucks,
Because all his deer looked like ducks.

Animals

or

How Mooge Went Wild Taming Animals

In the time of Mooge and wife,

There lived a range of wildlife.

All were savage, none yet tame,

Many made the tastiest game.

Now, one day, not far from home,

Mooge gnawed upon a tasty bone.

When up behind him, cool and calm,

A young wolf sneaked to his alarm.

Without his trusted flint-tipped spear,

Mooge froze and shook, consumed with fear.

He yelped a little and backed away.

The wolf edged closer, eyeing its prey.

Upon the ground Mooge found a stick.

With wolf in range, he aimed at it.

His throw was wide and flew beyond,

The wolf got ready to respond.

Our grown-up Mooge then cried for mum,

Dropped his bone and sucked his thumb.

But rather than pounce on our scaredy-cat man,

The wolf just barked, turned round, and ran.

Finding the stick, it picked it up,

Bounding back like an excited pup.

At Mooge's big feet it dropped the treat,

Wagging its tail and taking a seat.

So, Mooge retrieved the drool-wet wood,

Threatening the wolf as best he could.

But still it lingered, bouncing high.

Was this the end? Mooge feared he'd die.

He threw the stick and ran away,

As barking and howling mixed with a neigh.

It wasn't just the man it scared,

But a nearby horse, whose nostrils flared.

This wild, black mare then sprinted past,

And got Mooge's brain thinking quite fast.

With a run and a leap, he climbed atop

This galloping horse, who didn't stop,

But bolted and bucked to dislodge her rider,

Spooked and alarmed by the wolf behind her.

Still clinging tight, arms round her neck,

Mooge stayed astride, his nerves a wreck.

On they rode, over brook and shrub,

And all this time chased by the cub.

Until they arrived at a patch of grass,

When the mare slowed down to halt at last.

There, munching on the green, lush shoots,

Were sheep stirred by Mooge's shrieks and hoots.

The wolf, who spied its natural prey,

Forgot our Mooge and veered away.

It crept around the bleating flock,

Herding them into a tidy block.

Away in the distance our Flair gazed

Upon this scene that so amazed.

She hurried across, her legs moved quick,

As Mooge fell off and was promptly sick.

"Oh, that was great!" exclaimed our Flair,

The horse now calm, without a care.

"Each beast in sight we can control

With time and food fed in a bowl."

Our Mooge jumped up and shook his head.

"But that killer wolf wished me dead!

And did you see that crazy horse?"

To which Flair laughed without remorse.

"Oh, dear old Mooge, you're so naïve.

Just think of what we could achieve!

Our journeys will be nice and quick:

Though you'll still moan and then be sick.

We'll herd the sheep and use their wool.

The wolf can help just like a tool."

Mooge sighed and scratched his aching bum,

His brow confused, his mouth all glum.

"What's the matter?" asked Flair with a groan.

"Well," sobbed Mooge, "I've lost my bone!"

Although his bone was never found,

They soon tamed both the horse and hound.

For did you know, it is the case,

Your doggy of today can trace

Its family back to old Mooge's wolf?

And if you're after further proof,

Ask one if you can chew their bone,

Then hear them growl like Mooge would moan.

The Wheel

or

How Mooge Got Round to Inventing the Wheel

Mooge huffed and puffed with some regret.

He'd hoped that tools would save on sweat,

But now he knew it wasn't true.

They just made other work to do.

He swung his axe against a tree.

The impact was so hard to see.

"It's blunt!" cried Mooge, addressing Flair,

Then threw his hands up in despair.

But Flair insisted he chop it down,

And watched him with her favourite frown.

"Our neighbour Og now owns a door.

I want one too, plus a wooden floor!"

The wolf, named Dog, lay by Flair's feet,

Her ears alert for a distant bleat.

Flair fed her food and tickled her tum,
As poor Mooge hit both tree and thumb.

"Falymandosa&%$@!" he cried aloud
(At times like this poor grammar's allowed).
Dog paid no heed with a yawn and stretch:
Their new best friend who loved to fetch.
"This flint is blunt!" Mooge moaned again.
"My hands are hurting. I'm suffering pain."

He showed his palms, all covered in sores,

Breathing deep, as he paused his chores.

With pity for her husband's plight,

Flair whipped out gloves knitted one night.

"I made these from our sheepy's wool.

They're nice and soft and pretty cool."

Mooge put them on, and grinned in kind,

Then swung the axe with a curse in mind.

After many hours of sweat and blood,

The tree stood ready to fall and thud.

Never having chopped one quite so tall,

Mooge wondered which way the tree might fall.

He swung the axe with all his might.

The tree swayed left and then swayed right.

It fell his way, this eight-ton weight.

Flair screamed out "Run!", almost too late.

The panic and noise woke up Dog,
Who howled and barked at the log.
Now, one small thing I've yet to mention
At this time of unbearable tension,
Is our big tree grew atop a hill,
It crashed to earth and lay quite still. Until…
Down the slope it began to tumble,
Increasing speed with a roaring rumble.
As Mooge dashed off to escape the brute,
The trunk rolled down in hot pursuit.

Dog's tail wagged, she barked and followed.
"It's not a stick!" Flair now bellowed.
Mooge ran and ran as fast as he could,
But was soon outpaced by the piece of wood.
Facedown he lay, squished in the dirt.
Each bone and muscle ached with hurt.

Dog then stopped to lick Mooge's face,

While Flair's brain worked at faster pace.

"The tree moved like a stampeding blur,

Because its shape is circular!

If we could slice the tree in bits,

Link two pieces with a stick that fits

In the middle, at the circles' heart,

Then we will have a working… 'cart'!"

Mooge just groaned and brushed off muck,
Sitting up straight, cursing his luck.
For he understood when Flair said 'we'
That what she meant to say was 'he'!
So, Flair's idea changed their life,
Making things easier, removing the strife.
With wheel and axle, that most important part,
They could move large things with horse and cart,
From stones and wood, food and sheep,
And poor old Mooge when he fell asleep.

The Boat

or

How Mooge Got into Hot Water with The First Boat

Mooge and trees were not best of chums,

They gave him bruises, hurting his thumbs.

Yet the one thing Mooge hated more,

Was getting wet, which chilled his core.

He couldn't swim, tried not to wash,

And feared the beasts that went splish-splosh.

As the snows melted to mix with the rains,

Water was everywhere and they didn't have drains.

So, when Flair said, with a smiley face,

How trees could float on its surface,

Mooge cringed and hid upon the heath,

Until dragged back between Dog's teeth.

"If we carved out a mighty trunk,"

Said Flair, as she skinned a smelly skunk.

"Then we could travel both far and wide,

Down rivers, to islands and beyond the tide."

She whooped at the end, exciting young Dog,

But Mooge knew who would have to slog.

And so, as he thought, it came to be,

That he carved out the mighty tree.

Proud he was of those weeks of labour,

Bragging to Og, his rival neighbour.

Then came the day to launch their 'boat',

As Flair had named the things that float.

Family and friends all came to watch,

While Mooge finished off one final notch.

One half pulled on a length of rope,

The others pushed down the muddy slope,

Until it bobbed upon the river,

Upright and steady, with a gentle quiver.

The crowd all cheered and wished them well,

Except for Og, who let rip a smell.

Then in climbed Mooge and Flair with pride,

All ready for a pleasant ride.

But Flair went pale and said, "Oh, pet,

Explain to me why my feet are wet?"

Mooge blushed and gulped. They began to sink.

"I put a hole in so that we could drink."

An hour passed to fix Mooge's error.

Plenty of time to face his terror.

He ducked beneath to find the boat,

Feeling the pressure to make it re-float.

With all his strength, he tugged and twisted,

Until the log no longer resisted.

Ashore once more he fixed the hole,

With wool and dung shaped in a roll.

Flair's idea, as you'll have guessed,

She was rarely wrong; always knew best.

When Og had stopped his tears of laughter,

Flair tried again with Mooge behind her.

"Success!" she cried, aboard their craft,
Drifting along with a gentle draft.
And all was fine on their floating log,
Until Mooge stood up to moon at Og.

He wobbled, rocked, and let out a yell,
Waving his arms before he fell
Back in the water, headfirst in the muck,
As Flair rowed to shore, avoiding a duck.
(to be continued...)

Ceramics

or

How Mooge Went Potty with Pottery

With everyone watching, including a frog,
Mooge patiently waited for rescue by Dog.
The cold water bubbled, as they surfaced for air,
Mooge in Dog's teeth, with mud covered hair.

He wasn't much help to his canine friend,
Spluttering and lifted by his backend.
Once upon land, Dog opened her jaws,
Dropping her load, licking her paws.
Mooge sat up straight and squirted out slime,
Wiping his eyes to free them from grime.

Flair tapped her foot, ready to strike,
With language most fruity, not ladylike.
She ordered her hubby back to their home,
And there it was she started her moan.
"You're not coming in, all covered in goo!
I just cleaned this morning because of you!"
The pail of water was a little surprising.
"It's cold!" cried Mooge, goosebumps arising.

With all the mud gone, Flair narrowed her eyes,
Inspecting Mooge as he dried off his thighs.
His skin looked different, much softer, so young.
"It must be the mud," she mused with a hum.
Dabbing her cheek, with a blob on her nose,
She soon disappeared to clean up his clothes.
Then later that day, as Mooge took a nap,
Flair came home with a facial mudpack.

Mooge awoke, screaming out loud,
Alarming Dog, who barked and howled.
"Calm down, you fool! It's only me,"
Said Flair, as she washed her face mud-free.
She stroked her cheek with an open hand.
"I'm ten years younger, just as planned!"
Word then spread of the miracle of mud,
Of how it calmed and cooled the blood.
Soon their cave was a popular place
For people to come to cover their face.

Men said they came to experience the dirt,
Though it's common knowledge they came to shirk.
And women came calling, long in the tooth,
Wanting treatment to recapture their youth.
With dollops of sludge stacked by the food,
The cave looked different, confusing our Mooge.
He blamed the wolf for doing a pooh.
Dog eyed him back and snarled, "It was you!"
But knowing manure burns for so long,
Mooge used the fire to hide the pong.
It burned all night, and then came the morning,
When Flair wandered in stretching and yawning.
She noticed a lump, alone in the ash,
Picking it up to throw out as trash.

"Oh, Mooge, have you...?" her question began,
Before her brain struck on a plan.
The clay had changed, hardened, and set,
Shaped like a duck and coloured brunette.

"We'll hang this 'duck' up in our cave,"
Declared our Flair, as Mooge tried to shave.
As days passed by, she tried again,
Moulding the clay to bake in the flame.
With time and practice, and the odd mistake,
She finally cracked it and started to make
Some bowls and jugs and pretty pots.
Guess who got smothered in slimy spots?
"I don't like sludge and water less!"
Mooge grumbled out loud in a fine old mess.
Flair pottered on, ignoring his moan,
And with Mooge in mind, she invented the gnome.

Pickling and Preserving
Or
How it bugged Mooge he was Sick,
While Flair was Sick of Bugs

With horse to ride and wolf to hunt,

Their cart to pull and boat to punt,

Both Mooge and Flair travelled wide,

Following the food, their only guide.

Their bellies grew, their family too,

When Flair gave birth to their daughter, Croo.

For Mooge, she was his sun and light,

But kept him up most of the night.

He'd rock her back to sleep with song,

Changing her fur when it started to pong.

Then when she slept, he'd stay awake,

Pacing outside while thinking of steak.

On one such night, with all now silent,

Feeling his tummy's urgent requirement,

He tiptoed to their stash of food,

Which Flair thought safe from sly old Mooge.

He found a bowl of fruit and grain,

Left lying in the pouring rain.

It smelt quite odd but looked okay:

Mooge rarely turned food away.

With a noisy slurp and a mighty gulp,

He swallowed down the gloopy pulp.

It tasted nice and made him warm:

A lull before the coming storm.

For soon his breath tasted of flames.

He coughed and wheezed, with burning pains,

Staggering around, gripping his throat,

Crashing and banging until Flair awoke.

"What have you done!" cried she aloud,

Surprised and aghast at the scene around.

Mooge swayed and slurred his every word,
The world now spinning, the walls all blurred.

"I drank ssshomefing from the bowl,
And now my limbsssh have losssht control!"
Flair growled and huffed, not best amused.
She didn't like this thing called booze.
When all the noise awoke their Croo,
She kicked Mooge out with words most blue.
The bowl from which he'd not long drunk,
Still lay about, and worse, it stunk!
Flair wiped it with a surly swish,
"Hang on! No mould grows in this dish?"

Now, this was odd given its old age,

When most food rotted by this stage.

"Perhaps this mixture possesses some powers,

Keeping things clean and fresh for hours?"

And so was born this brilliant find,

To kill the germs that plague our kind.

Flair waited until the morning light,

To tell Mooge of her breakthrough night.

She found him laying among the sheep,

Snoring out loud and deep asleep.

"Get up!" Flair chose to shout each word,

Loud and clear to ensure Mooge heard.

It worked a treat, as was plain,

As Mooge awoke with an aching brain.

He wailed and groaned, "Make it stop!
I'll never touch another drop."
With Flair still nagging in his ear,
Mooge shuffled off to get well clear.
He found Dog sleeping by some trees,
And slumped back down upon his knees.
Rubbing his eyes, with their pounding throb,
Mooge rested his head on the hair of Dog.

The fleas who lived within Dog's fur,
Were not amused by the unwelcome stir.
They hopped away from Mooge's foul breath
Which stank of booze and promised death.
But soon Mooge snored out loud again,
Dreaming of steak and hunting game.
As years passed by, Mooge kept his word
Despite what stories you may have heard.
It was Flair who brewed a jar or two,
To kill the bugs that prompt the loo.
In every drink she dropped a drip,
So, all drank safe with every sip.

And then she learned to pickle fruits,

And other things like eggs and roots.

Preserved in wine for wintertime

So, when things were hard all could dine.

For in moderation, and used with sense,

Alcohol has been immense,

In helping to shape humankind.

A valuable lesson to keep in mind.

Bread

or

How Mooge Didn't Use his Loaf to Help Make Bread

Mooge's empty stomach groaned and grumbled,

As he looked across the plain and mumbled.

Not a single beast had he caught for days,

All tucked up safe in their hideaways.

To calm his hunger and make it pass,

Mooge plucked the heads off nearby grass,

And chewed upon their chalky seed:

A trifle bland but it met a need.

He picked some more for his dear wife.

This lack of meat would cause some strife.

Then set off home with Og and Pel,

Whose arrows and spears had missed as well.

They hardly talked with a sullen mood,

But when they did it was coarse and crude.

And as expected, when they made it home,
Flair greeted them with an angry moan.
She threw the seeds, as poor Mooge fled.
Best not to write what our dear Flair said.
So, hiding the seeds beneath a stone,
Mooge sat upon it to sulk alone.
The rock was hard, he began to fidget,
Turning and twisting like a cornered piglet.

At last, he stood, adjusting his seat,
Finding powder where once was wheat.
The seeds had all been ground to dust.
He cursed the world that was so unjust.
Then jumped in fury, up and down,
Crying and wailing to all around.
Crashing to earth, the husks bounced away,
Leaving the powder just where it lay.
As Mooge ranted and threw out his toys,
Flair hurled cold water to stop all his noise.

A splash or two mixed with the powder,
Turning it gloopy, more like chowder.
Ignoring her hubby, Flair got out a bowl,
And scooped it up from the shallow hole.
It lacked a little, so she added some fat,
Plus a drop of milk, and rolled it flat
Then laid it out on a cooking stone,
As Mooge looked on, chewing his bone.

"It's a test," Flair explained, watching the fire,

"We only learn if we try and enquire."

After several minutes upon their stove,

Flair retrieved the treasure from its trove,

Then cut the loaf with a slither of stone,

And offered to Mooge to replace his bone.

Mooge took a bite, sighed and uttered,

"This would be better with jam and buttered!"

Farming

or

How Mooge helped Flair plant the seed of an idea

In summer days, when snows had thawed,
Mooge had no time to claim, "I'm bored!"
With family in tow, they trekked afar,
Following the herds under moon and star.

Hunting by day and tracking by night.
A tiresome life and Mooge looked a sight,
With bags under eyes and hair all a mess.
He moaned to Flair with his usual excess.
"I miss my cave and the comforts of home,"
Before taking a chew on a tasty bone.

Now Flair, no less busy and no less tired,
Considered this problem as her brow perspired.
Food was the reason they roamed with a moan.
If only it would stay far closer to home.
Then on one day, while gathering seed,
Flair remembered a time when she'd
Found some wheat at this very same place,
Making Mooge bread to stuff his face.
With seed left over, she'd thrown it away.
Now on that spot there grew grain today.
That brain of hers soon worked it out.
"I've got it!" she declared with a shout.
"We'll take the seed with us to sow,
Near our cave to watch them grow.
We'll build a fence to hold the sheep.
So, grain for us and hay to keep
The sheepy fed when winter comes.
That's food at hand to fill our tums."

Now Mooge's dim mind was on his bone,
And all he heard was a garbled drone.
So, when time came to pack up camp,
To ready the horse for a long, hard tramp,
And Flair asked Mooge to collect the grain,
Our loveable hero turned off his brain.
He loaded a yard of turf on the cart,
Waking up Dog with a call to depart.

Dog just barked and sniffed at the scene,
Of stalks on the cart with soil in-between.
It stirred our Flair to inspect Mooge's work,
Causing a gasp at the expense of her berk.
"What are you doing?" she demanded of Mooge.
"Didn't you hear me advise on our food?"
Mooge scratched his head, clearly confused.
"I did," he answered, his brain-cells all used.
"Now we have food wherever we go,
By lugging these stalks to-and-fro.
I'll call this method a 'take-away'.
Pretty neat, eh? What do you say?"

Flair kept her thoughts to herself,
Breathing deep for the sake of her health.
This 'take-away' thing would never catch on.
I'll leave it to you to decide if she was wrong.
Back near their cave, Mooge cleared some land,
Cutting down trees, just as Flair planned.

When the soil was soft, she planted the seeds
Watering often, removing the weeds.
They watched them grow, tall and strong,
Until things went terribly wrong.
Mooge, in charge of the new sheep pen,
Opened the gate as he chased a hen.
The sheep escaped, finding the crop,
And started to munch: chomp, chomp, chop.

Dog spotted the danger, saving the wheat

Herding them back, those naughty sheep!

As a reward, Mooge built Dog a hut.

Mooge's punishment? He had to live with the mutt!

Writing

or

How Mooge Getting Things Wrong, Made Flair Write

As years passed by and all grew old,
They sat round fires where tales got told,
Of those difficult times back in the day,
Before horses, clothes, fire, or clay.
Good food was scarce, and hunger common,
And life too short for every human.

When Mooge departed, hunting for hare,
He moaned, "Missing the stories just isn't fair!"
Flair thought about poor Mooge's frustration
And how best to keep some information.
With food they reaped from their labours
Now traded for goods made by their neighbours,
A record was needed to make things fair:
Of whom owed what and what went where.

And when they'd died, like Pel and Dog,
Would their stories fade just like the fog?
They'd learned too much to let it go,
Lost and forgotten like melted snow.
Flair wanted to celebrate what she'd done,
From having nothing to becoming a mum.
How Croo now helped out on the farm,
Picking the wheat, building a barn.
Of how her boy, Nooge, herded the goats,
Hunting with dad and painting the boats.
And how they no longer had to roam,
As they lived in a substantial home,
Of wattle and daub, with a hearth and fire,
And clay ducks on the wall to admire.

(Don't write them a letter, I must now stress,

As they don't have post, nor an address).

The ice had crept back in retreat,

The climate warmer, meaning more to eat.

There was only one thing that remained the same.

Guess who? Always in trouble: always to blame.

Mooge still got into all types of scrapes,

Running from bears, sitting on snakes.

And still he moaned and avoided chores,

Eating too much, gorging on boars.

But despite his habit of coming unstuck,

He still inspired Flair by good luck.

For she found some clay, a little wet,

To draw upon, so they'd never forget.

With lines she recorded bushels of wheat,

And with crosses, how much Mooge would eat.

To remember Dog she marked her grave,

And on Uncle Pel's she drew a wave.

She wrote a symbol for everyone,

From Mooge and Croo, to their god, the Sun.

But when Mooge missed a campfire tale,

Flair's wonderful writing was doomed to fail.

The one thing needed for it to succeed,

Was for foolish Mooge to learn to read.

Too lazy and distracted by his sheep,

He missed his lessons or fell asleep.

And, so, he could never read or write,

When everyone can, with support that's right.

Now, can you imagine how that must be?

You wouldn't have enjoyed this great story!

And on this note our tale ends,

As we bid goodbye to all our friends.

Prehistory, that age of mystery,

Moves forward into history,

For when they learned to read and write,

Our ancestors left their lives in plain sight,

For people like us to find and study:

The past became much less muddy.

But let's not forget what was done

By those at the start for everyone.

Whose names and deeds we may never know,

Except our Flair, Dog and co.

And don't forget one special dude,

That prehistoric genius called Mooge!

If you enjoyed the adventures of Mooge and Flair then let your friends know about it and ask your parents to leave an online review somewhere.

Thank you,

Nate

Timeline and Facts

Mooge's and Flair's adventures are, of course, make-believe. In the time called prehistory (before writing and the recording of events), it is impossible to say who invented or discovered anything. However, archaeologists, who study really old things, can provide estimates for when certain events took place from objects they find buried in the ground, like bones and flints.

Our ancient ancestors would have made improvements to their lives through necessity, as climates changed, and they adapted to survive. Such changes and improvements took many, many years to come about, perhaps with a stroke of good luck or an accident along the way. Inventions, like tools and the control of fire, helped humans eat a better, more varied diet, which in turn helped with physical improvements. As the human population slowly increased and families travelled longer distances in search of food and safety, they shared ideas and techniques with others, leading to further improvements. Sometimes the same idea or invention emerged in a few different places around the world independently at different times, such as writing. So, there are an awful lot of 'Mooges' and 'Flairs' to thank!

Check out the timeline showing when we believe humans developed all the wonderful things mentioned in Mooge.

Now, pick one of the inventions or discoveries from this book and try to imagine what your life would be like if it never existed, or humans never learned to controlled it!

Discover other fun resources to help learn about prehistory on Mooge's website: www.moogeprehistoricgenius.com

Some archeologists think hominis used fire in Africa as far back as 1.5 million years ago. However, there is no hard evidence humans could control fire until about 400,000 years ago.

Evidence of the first stone tools found in Africa dated to 3.3 million years ago.

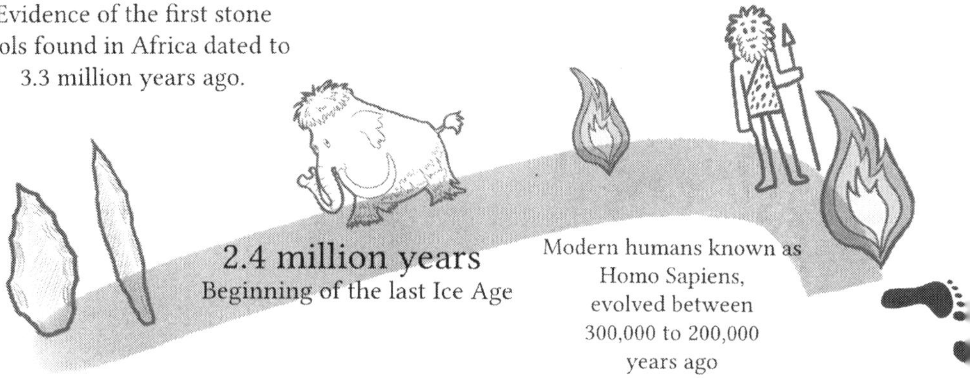

2.4 million years
Beginning of the last Ice Age

Modern humans known as Homo Sapiens, evolved between 300,000 to 200,000 years ago

The first evidence of bread and farming coincide at the same time in the Middle East around 10,000 years ago. Before this time, humans lived a nomadic life as hunter-gatherers. Caves would not have been permanent homes, just convenient places to stay at certain times of the year.

The first wheels were made from wood and the first wheeled vehicles appeared in the Middle East and Eastern Europe about 5,600 years ago. They would not have been much use without the invention of the axle too.

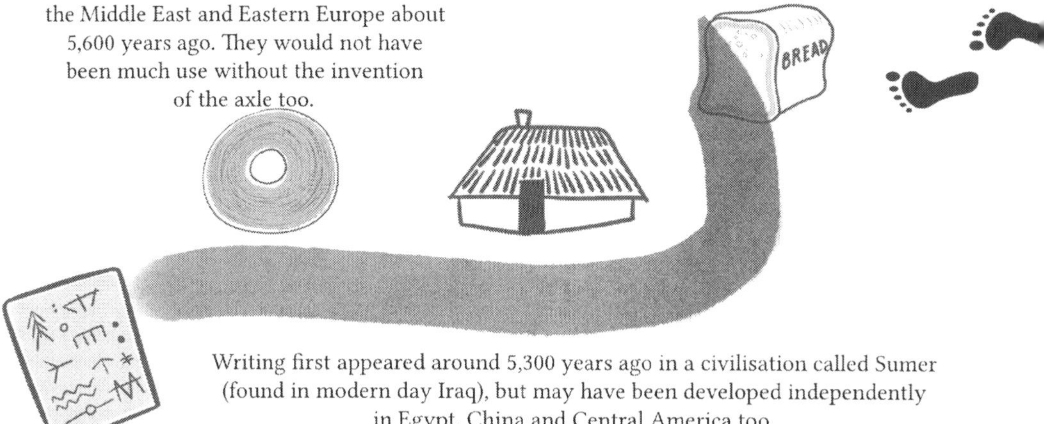

Writing first appeared around 5,300 years ago in a civilisation called Sumer (found in modern day Iraq), but may have been developed independently in Egypt, China and Central America too.

By studying body lice, scientists think clothes were first worn around 170,000 years ago. They believe body lice evolved from head lice at this date when they found a new home in clothing.

The earliest form of ceramics, dated to 26,000 years ago, were found in what is today the Czech Republic and include objects in the shape of animals and human figures.

The oldest evidence of brewed beer was found in modern day Israel. However, because alcohol occurs naturally, as rotting, fermenting fruit, it is believed humans may have been drinking it for millions of years.

The oldest and best surviving art has been found in caves and includes handprints created by spitting paint from the mouth. They would have used ground earth pigments mixed with water.

End of last Ice Age

The earliest depiction of a boat is from a 12,000 year old carving in modern day Azerbaijan. However, some believe sea-worthy boats could have been around from as early as 800,000 years ago, explaining how early humans reached certain parts of the world where their tools have been found.

The first domestication of animals took place in South West Asia between 11,000 and 13,000 years ago. Sheep and dogs are thought to be the first animals domesticated by humans.

| PYRAMIDS BUILT 4650 YEARS | PAPER 2200 YEARS | PRINTING PRESS 580 YEARS | FIRST FLIGHT BY WRIGHT BROTHERS | NOW |
| IRON AGE 3300 YEARS | GUNPOWDER 1200 YEARS | STEAM ENGINE 315 YEARS | MOON LANDING 53 YEARS | |

About the Author

Nate Wrey is old and hairy like Uncle Pel but not as smelly. Unlike Mooge, he paid attention at school and learned to read and write. *Mooge: The Prehistoric Genius* is his first children's book. He learned all about history at school and university.

When he was young, Nate liked books by Roald Dahl, which are fun and exciting, with great characters who get in and out of trouble, teaching valuable lessons as a result. He also enjoyed reading cartoons such as Asterix the Gaul, starting his interest in history.

Nate has a day job as a Civil Servant, working for the government, but has also written a novel for adults (as Nathaniel M Wrey) called *Liberty Bound*, which won a Readers' Favorite International Book Award in 2021. He lives in Kent with ceramic ducks on his walls.

For more info visit
www.moogeprehistoricgenius.com

Printed in Great Britain
by Amazon